Daring Deeds - World War II Short Stories for Kids

Family-Friendly Stories About Friendship, Bravery, Kindness & Love for 8-14 Year Olds

KLG History

Published by KLG History

Copyright © 2023 by KLG History

All rights reserved.

No part of this book may be reproduced in any form or by any electronic or mechanical means, including information storage and retrieval systems, without written permission from the author, except for the use of brief quotations in a book review.

Cover design courtesy of 99Designs.com (Design Agreement Available from the Publisher on Request)

Bluberry-Normal Typeface License Purchased from CreativeMarket.com on April 4th, 2023- Order Number 135067108

Print ISBN: 978-1-915363-55-8

Contents

Introduction	v
1. The Dutch Farmer	1
2. Mientjes Unbreakable Spirit	6
3. The Syrian Bear	11
4. Friendly Fire	16
5. An Answered Prayer	22
6. A Loving Reunion	26
7. The Spirit of Christmas	31
8. Music of the Night	36
9. A Sailor's Best Friend	40
10. Moral Victory	45
11. The City of Forgiveness	50
12. Judy	55
13. The Sugihara Visas	61
14. Night Flight	66
15. The Parachute	68
16. Good Gruber	75
17. The Volksdeutsche	80
18. The Warrior Women	85
19. A Better Scientist	90
20. Airdrop from Above	95
Conclusion	101
Also by KLG History	103

Introduction

World War II began on the 1st of September 1939, when Hitler ordered German troops to attack Poland - and lasted all the way until the 2nd of September 1945, when surrender documents were officially signed by Japan. This was a terrifying, difficult, and heart-breaking time, but amongst the evil intentions, death, and despair that many endured - there were some inspiring tales of heroism, courage, friendship and love to come out of it. Inside this book you'll get to read and reflect on 20 of these rarely told, but wonderful tales from around the Globe. They'll inspire hope and teach lessons that are important for all children (and adults) to know.

They can be applied and will make a difference in our everyday life and to those around us - even if we aren't parachuting out of planes or sailing on war ships behind enemy lines to do it.

Introduction

We hope you enjoy these short stories from WWII.

Chapter 1

The Dutch Farmer

In the spring of 1940, six months after the start of the Second World War, Hitler's armies made swift, targeted attacks on the Low Countries of Western Europe. They conquered Belgium, Luxembourg, and the Netherlands and then took France within a matter of weeks.

Despite the Netherlands wanting no part in the war and declaring itself neutral, the Nazi invasion of the country began on 10 May, and, though the Dutch fought hard against the German forces, on 14 May 1940, they had little choice but to surrender.

It was a frightening time for the population. After the Nazi invasion of Poland in 1939, the Poles were subjected to cruel and brutal treatment, and all their resources were plundered. Everything of value was taken by Germany. The Dutch people were well aware of this and feared they were facing the same fate, but

Hitler viewed the Dutch very differently from the Slavs of central and Eastern Europe; he saw them as fellow Aryans (the racial category of white, non-Jewish people Hitler considered superior) and aimed to cooperate with the Dutch Government - then gradually introduce his new laws and policies in the hope that this 'Germanic brother nation' would come to accept Nazism. By the end of the war, however, Nazi Germany controlled every aspect of Dutch society; the economy, education, culture, and the media, with freedom of speech and expression abolished.

The German occupation of the Netherlands was known as *De Bezetting*. On the whole, the Dutch population was very unhappy about the situation, their royal family had fled to Britain, and it was humiliating being ruled by their aggressive neighbors even though most of the countries of Europe were in the same boat. The majority in the Netherlands hated the Germans but believed they had no option but to reluctantly comply with the new regime. Some (about five percent) formed a Resistance and made every effort to undermine German rule, particularly after the first round-up of Dutch Jews in February 1941.

But resisting the Germans was risky business. The death penalty in the Netherlands had been abolished in the previous century, so the public were shocked and bewildered when the Nazis began executing resistors that they had arrested. Despite this, there were many ordinary Dutch people who risked everything to help Jews (and others) in hiding from German persecution.

In the beginning, life was not as bad as they had feared, and there were certainly more jobs available - building German defenses and manufacturing, but as time passed, there was little for the workers to spend their wages on since barely anything could be imported into the country.

As food became scarcer in the larger cities, the German occupiers introduced a new system to distribute the food that was available fairly throughout the country, so farms were forced to hand over all their produce and harvests. It was extra unwanted pressure for the Dutch farmers and agricultural laborers, who had continued to work the land while the war raged on.

Many farm horses had been requisitioned by the German army for its mounted cavalry or to haul the heavy artillery guns, and consequently, farm workers were often left having to plow fields and transport vegetables and grain using methods similar to those used by medieval peasants five hundred years earlier!

One young farmer, Toon Graumans, was one of the lucky ones who had managed to keep hold of his horses. His farm was at Etten-Leur, a village in the North Brabant province in the south of the Netherlands. One day, in 1944, he was working hard, preparing the soil in one of his fields that was close to the railway. He didn't pay much attention to a freight train trundling slowly along the line, as he was busy concentrating on the task at hand when his horses suddenly stopped and raised their heads. Irritated and impatient to finish, Toon tried to encourage them to continue when he realized that they had been alerted by a man, standing right there in his field.

He could see that this stranger was filthy, dressed in ragged old clothes that were full of holes, and he couldn't have washed or shaved in days. He put his arm up and waved. Toon did not react but continued his work as he gathered his thoughts and made another circuit of the large field with his horses. As he returned to where he had first noticed the man, he found five more waiting there. They were in just the same state, dirty and disheveled, and as he drew closer, Toon could make out that they were all wearing handcuffs.

He quickly surmised that they must be prisoners of war who had escaped from the slow train that had passed by earlier, but what should he do? Six fugitives on his land; if he didn't hand them over and the Nazi overlords found out, he would be in serious trouble. They could deport him to do forced labor or to one of the concentration camps he had heard rumors about- or worse. But these men must be desperate and frightened, and what would happen to them if he didn't help?

He made up his mind and brought them some bread and fresh milk. The men ate hungrily, and it was deli-

4

cious after the meager rations they were used to as prisoners. Toon was wondering what more he could do for them when his neighbor arrived unexpectedly.

Could he be trusted? In wartime, people often behaved out of character and betrayed anyone they found breaking the rules, scared that they might be implicated if they didn't, or hoping they might find favor for themselves and their families with the occupying forces. Toon decided to take a risk and explained how he had found these unexpected guests on his land. To his relief, this neighbor was sympathetic, and between them, they managed to conceal the fugitives and make contact with local members of the Resistance. Very soon, arrangements were made, and the six men were on their way to freedom.

Toon never forgot the gratitude shown by those poor, wretched prisoners and never regretted his decision. His village was liberated by American soldiers from the 104th Infantry Division towards the end of October 1944, and Toon continued to farm his fertile Dutch land in peacetime. He often wondered if those six men did manage to survive the war. He never knew who they were or where they were from, but he remained satisfied that he, when the opportunity arose, had resisted Hitler's evil regime and helped those in real need.

Chapter 2

Mientjes Unbreakable Spirit

Bergen op Zoom is an old city in the southwest of the Netherlands with a rich history. In 1940, Hitler's forces invaded the country, and Bergen op Zoom, along with the rest of the country, was subjected to years of Nazi occupation.

One of the city's inhabitants, Mientje Proost, was nineteen when her brother, Louis, was arrested for his involvement with the local Resistance. Not long afterward, one of his friends approached her to ask if she would deliver a package for the group. Although life was hard under the occupation and everyone hated being under the oppressive, strict rule of the Nazis, Mientje did not have particularly strong political views; she was more interested in planning her future - her dream was to become a nurse, but she wanted to help her brother's friends, so she agreed to take the package and become a courier.

Resistance groups were formed to give vital intelligence information to the Allies and to help servicemen or agents who found themselves behind enemy lines. They also undertook sabotage missions, anything to get rid of the Nazis and prepare for their country's liberation. These groups, known as networks, relied on couriers to carry incriminating documents or escort fugitives who were in danger of being arrested. They were usually young women who the Nazis were less likely to suspect to be members of an underground paramilitary unit, but it was still very dangerous work; couriers operated in full view of the Germans, and there was the risk that neighbors who noticed any unusual behavior might inform the authorities, and almost anything could go wrong on a mission.

Mientje called her packages *kaas* (cheese), and they contained faked documents, identity and ration cards, and papers that included microdots (a microphotograph, often of a map, plans, or instructions that measured just one millimeter squared). She traveled by train to the neighboring towns of Bussum and Haarlem to deliver her *kaas* parcels as a valuable member of the *Dienst Wim* Dutch Resistance network.

In the summer of 1943, Anton van der Waals joined the network. Unbeknown to the resistors, he was a collaborator who was helping the enemy, and as soon as he had identified all of the *Dienst Wim* resistors, they were all arrested between 24 July and 5 August

1943. Mientje was at her parent's shop on Zuivelstraat, in the center of Bergen op Zoom, when they came for her.

Mientje showed incredible bravery. She was interrogated by the Gestapo (the Geheime Staatspolizei, known as the Gestapo, was Nazi Germany's secret police), well known for their ruthless and cruel methods, but she refused to tell them anything.

Her captors sent her to a detention center in Scheveningen called the *Oranjehotel*, where she was held in isolation for seven months, but it did not break her. She drew on inner strength, and every day she got up, washed, cleaned her cell, and exercised, she found this routine helped her to build her mental strength, and she continued to withstand the regular interrogations she was subjected to.

When the Gestapo realized that questioning Mientje was useless, they sent her to the prison at Haaren. There, with little regard for her own life, she communicated with her fellow prisoners through the cell walls, a dentist on one side and an optician on the other, singing protest songs, including the *parachutistenlied* (parachute song), which was strictly forbidden.

On 21 June 1944, Mientje and other members of the *Dienst Wim* Resistance network were tried for crimes against their Nazi overlords at Haaren and sentenced to death, but she didn't give up hope. She believed her country would be liberated and that she would be saved...

The Nazi authorities sent her to Herzogenbusch concentration camp (in the Dutch town of Vught), where she was held as a political prisoner, then to the German camps of Ravensbrück and finally Dachau, and at each, Mientje stood up for her fellow prisoners, demanding better food and conditions, she even sang one of her protest songs when she met with the Commander of Dachau.

In 1944, the Allied forces landed at Normandy, and once they had liberated France, they battled to free the rest of the countries under Nazi occupation and moved toward the Netherlands. Hitler ordered forced evacuations of the concentration camps, a regime known as the 'death marches' in order to stop the thousands of prisoners from falling into the hands of the Allies. When Mientje heard that she and all her fellow inmates were to be herded south, under armed guard, she pleaded with the *commandant* of the camp to show some mercy and let them go, but he refused. Frustrated, she did what she could to prepare everyone, stealing bandages and medicines ready for the long and grueling trek ahead of them.

The marching columns left Dachau on 23 April 1945, and many prisoners, weak from disease, lack of food, or exhaustion, did not survive.

But Mientje made it. After she had been liberated, she was interviewed by the American intelligence agencies, and she was able to provide important information about the concentration camps and some of the cruel crimes committed by Nazi officials. After volunteering with the Red Cross for a short time, she finally returned to her home in May of 1945.

Throughout her captivity, Mientje never gave up hope, even in her darkest hours; she remained strong and determined. However, her experiences did come at a cost, she would never fully regain her health after enduring months of cruelty and hardship at the hands of her captors in the concentration camps, but her story of resilience and courage has been an inspiration to all who knew her.

Chapter 3

The Syrian Bear

Animals served in many different roles in the Second World War; horses hauled heavy guns to battlefronts, dogs were used as scouts to lead troops through enemy territory, and even pigeons played a part, delivering messages behind enemy lines, but one of the most unusual stories of animals at war must be that of Wojtek, the bear.

In April 1942, the Polish Anders' Army was evacuated from the Soviet Union (where it had been formed) and headed for Palestine. During this long journey, the soldiers passed through the Zagros mountains in Iran. There, they came across a young boy carrying an underfed Syrian bear cub he had found. Its mother had been shot by hunters, and he offered it to some of the soldiers in return for food.

Lieutenant Anatol Tarnowieck decided his unit, the 22nd Transport Company in the Artillery Division, would keep and raise the bear; the Anders Army had been raised from Poles who'd already had a difficult war. They had been deported from their homes and imprisoned in Russian gulags in the early stages and had no idea what had happened to their homes and families. He thought this lovable mascot might have a calming influence on his men and help build their morale.

The brown bear cub was given the old Slavic name Wojtek (pronounced' voy-tek'), meaning 'joyful warrior,' and the bear was appointed a guardian, Corporal Piotr Prendysz. The men took turns feeding him diluted condensed milk from an old vodka bottle, and it soon became clear that he was becoming much more to them than a mascot.

By the time they reached Palestine, Wojtek had grown into a mischievous little character. He liked to start each day with a shot of coffee, he enjoyed playfully wrestling with the men, drinking beer, and he would always join in if he saw a football game. He could salute, he liked to catch oranges, and there are even anecdotes of him stealing a washing line of underwear from a company of servicewomen and smoking cigarettes (which he ate afterward). The company moved to Alexandria, Egypt, and began to get ready to go to war.

When the 22nd Transport Company learned they were to be shipped to Italy to help fight against the German army, they learned that mascots and pets were forbidden on British troopships, but there was no question of them leaving their friend behind, so they enlisted Wojtek into the army as an honorary soldier. He was given the rank of private and issued with a pay book; his 'pay'? A double food ration!

In Italy, Private Wojtek, the 'soldier bear,' lived with the other men in tents, often keeping them warm when it was cold at night. His unit was tasked with delivering ammunition to the soldiers fighting in the Battle of Monte Cassino, one of the most brutal battles of the Second World War. The clever bear watched the men unloading empty ammunition crates from their trucks so they could be refilled and wanted to help. He was soon carrying empty crates and even loading guns, it has been said.

He always loved to ride in the cab of the ammunition truck, and he became a familiar sight to the Allied soldiers stationed in Italy. He always enjoyed a sweet treat. His favorites were fruit, honey, and marmalade. Once, hunting for jam, he devastated the food store while his company was celebrating a traditional Polish feast.

After the Allies had taken Monte Cassino, Wojtek served in just the same way, supporting the troops at the Battle of Bologna in the spring of 1945, and then the War in Europe ended. 2,000 Polish troops were shipped to a huge camp at Winfield airfield in Berwickshire, Scotland, and Wojtek, now promoted to the rank of Corporal, went with them. The people there adored him almost as much as his comrades did. Children loved to see him and sit on his back. He became somewhat of a local celebrity and even made appearances at organized dances.

Gradually, the soldiers began to leave the camp to get on with the rest of their lives. But what would become of Corporal Wojtek? Poland had been liberated from German occupation by Soviet forces, but Stalin installed a puppet government and brought it under Soviet rule. Most of the Polish servicemen who fought alongside the Western Allies (Britain and the USA) were devastated and were never able to return to their country. They did not want Wojtek to be sent east to become a symbol of the Soviet victory, so the big brown bear was de-mobbed to Edinburgh Zoo on 15 November 1947, where he remained a firm favorite until he died at the age of twenty-one in 1963. By the time of his death, he weighed nearly 500 kg (1,100lb) and was over 1.8 meters (5ft 11in) tall. His keeper said that he was a very quiet and peaceful character who loved to hear Polish voices though he had taken a dislike to a monkey and another bear that had also been adopted by troops.

Wojtek the bear will never be forgotten by the Polish Army; the insignia of the 22nd Transport Company now depicts a bear carrying an ammunition crate and his large, bronze memorial statue, with its paw pointing towards the figure of the Polish Army's Commanding Officer, General Wladyskaw Anders, proudly stands in Jordan Park in Krakow, Poland. His memory lives on in Scotland, too; another bronze Wojtek commemorating the courage of all Polish soldiers in the Second World War was unveiled in Edinburgh in November 2015. But, for those who served alongside him, he was more than an unusual mascot or a symbol of bravery; he was a true friend and comrade at a time of danger, uncertainty, and fear.

Chapter 4

Friendly Fire

On the morning of 20 December 1943, almost the entire US Air Force's 8th bomb group set out on a mission to destroy the Focke-Wulf aircraft manufacturing plant on the outskirts of Bremen in northern Germany. It would be dangerous; the plant would be well guarded with more than 250 anti-aircraft guns in the city and more than five hundred Lüftwaffe fighters, FW-190s, and BF-109s ready to defend the target.

Charles' Charlie' Lester Brown, a young pilot from Weston, West Virginia, would be on that raid. He served with the 527th Bombardment Squadron of the 379th Bombardment Group stationed at RAF Kimbolton in Cambridgeshire, England. It was to be his first mission on the B-17F Flying Fortress' named 'Ye Olde Pub.' His crew consisted of his co-pilot, 2nd Lieutenant Spencer G 'Pinky' Luke, his Navigator, 2nd

Lieutenant Albert A 'Doc' Sadok, Radio Operator and Bombardier 2nd Lieutenant Robert M 'Andy' Andrews, Top Turret Gunner Sergeant Bertrand O 'Frenchy' Coulombe, Radio Operator Sergeant Richard A 'Dick' Perchout, Tail Gunner Sergeant Hugh S 'Ecky' Eckenrode, Left Waist Gunner Sergeant Lloyd Jennings, Right Waist Gunner Sergeant Alex 'Russian' Yelesanko and finally Ball Turret Gunner Sergeant Samuel W 'Blackie' Blackford. Each man had a specific role in the aircraft, and they were ready to do their duty.

The American bombers set off. Charlie Brown had been expecting to be on the edge of the formation in a position known as 'Purple Heart Corner' because enemy guns tended to aim at the aircraft at the edges rather than those in the center, but three other bombers developed mechanical problems and had to turn back so 'the Pub' was ordered to move to the front of the formation.

The bombers crossed the North Sea and crossed the German border just after 11h00.

The German anti-aircraft flak guns opened fire, and suddenly, an explosion rocked The Pub - they had been hit. The plexiglass nose of the plane was shattered, and freezing cold air rushed into the cockpit. The anti-aircraft guns continued firing, and The Pub was hit again, disabling engine number 2. And another, this shell drove right through the left wing and then exploded, damaging engine 4; Charlie battled with everything he had to keep control of his aircraft.

But another shell tore through the roof! Charlie just about managed to keep The Pub straight when the radio command came through; it was time to drop the bombs. The bombardiers dropped their twelve 500lb bombs onto the target, and, mission accomplished; it was time to get back.

The Pub, seriously damaged, fell back from the formation. Charlie saw another B-17 (also hit by German flak and now on fire) dive in an attempt to extinguish the flames. Otherwise, the skies were clear.

Suddenly, his co-pilot, *Pinky*, pointed out a group of German fighter planes, Focke-Wulf 190s, determinedly advancing towards them and, where the other fighter had been, several Messerschmitt 109s. Charlie's men fired their machine guns, but Charlie quickly turned his aircraft, surprising the attackers, then flew at full speed towards the lead 190. *Frenchy's* bullets hit it, and it went down.

Then, the 109s began to close in. *Ecky*, the tail gunner, couldn't fire - the icy winds had frozen the oil in his machine gun. Charlie maneuvered The Pub sharply as it was sprayed by enemy bullets, piercing its ball turret (under the plane) and cutting through the tail rudder.

This attack left the aircraft with only two of its four engines operational; *Ecky*, the tail gunner, had been killed, *Dick* and *Russian* had both received severe shrapnel wounds, *Blacky's* electrically heated uniform had short-circuited and his feet had frozen, and a shell fragment had hit *Charlie* in the shoulder. The crew members that hadn't been injured could do little to help, the morphine vials that they carried were frozen; the radio had been destroyed. They decided against bailing out, *Russian* was too badly wounded, and they would have to leave him on the plane. Charlie began to lose consciousness, and The Pub dived.

As they descended downwards towards the city of Oldenburg, a burst of oxygen at the lower altitude quickly revived the pilot. At just 3,000 feet, Charlie managed to regain control and pulled The Pub back up.

Unable to pass speeds of 135mph and approaching Germany's border, where Hitler had positioned his best defenses, the outlook looked grim.

The Pub limped on over Jever Airfield, where German fighter ace Franz Stigler was refueling and rearming his Messerschmitt Bf-109. He quickly took off and approached The Pub, ready to attack, but as he neared his target, wondering why it hadn't fired at him, he was astonished to see the extent of the damage the aircraft had suffered, then through the ripped open sections of its frame, he could see the desperate crew.

The words of one of his commanding officers during his service in North Africa came to Franz, "If I ever see or hear of you shooting at a man coming down in a parachute, I will shoot you myself!" And he realized the stricken crew were just as vulnerable. He flew alongside the cockpit and tried to catch Charlie's attention.

Charlie, focused on flying his ailing aircraft, suddenly saw the Messerschmitt beside him. Franz waved and pointed downwards, telling him to land, but there was no chance of that; the German anti-aircraft defenses would obliterate The Pub if they opened fire on it.

Franz knew they had little chance of surviving unless he helped, so knowing the anti-aircraft gunners on the ground would recognize his fighter escorting the American bomber and hold their fire, he continued to fly alongside.

Charlie couldn't understand what he was doing. Why hadn't he fired? He ordered his gunners to point their guns in Franz's direction but not to shoot. He could see Franz gesturing and mouthing something, but the message wasn't clear. The German pilot was trying to point Charlie in the direction of neutral Sweden, where he could attempt a safe landing.

As The Pub finally left enemy airspace, Franz saluted and turned back. Charlie finally realized how lucky he had been that Franz had guarded them against being shot down. For his part, as soon as Franz had seen how vulnerable they were, wounded and desperate in the wrecked aircraft said, "To me, it was just like they had been in a parachute." He never told anyone anything about that flight, knowing the Lüftwaffe would take a very dim view of a pilot sparing the enemy whilst in combat.

Charlie managed to fly across the North Sea and back to Britain and landed at RAF Seething. He told his officers about the extraordinary incident during his debriefing, but he was warned to keep it quiet; it would be very dangerous for other aircraft to assume German fighter pilots would treat them in the same way.

Ye Olde Pub never flew again; it was shipped back to the States and scrapped. The two pilots continued their service until the end of the war; Franz was a Me-262 jet fighter pilot in Jagdverband 44, and Charlie completed a combat tour.

More than forty years after the war had ended, Charlie retired from an illustrious career in government service and wondered what had happened to his enemy guardian. After four years of searching, he received a letter from Franz, who had seen one of Charlie's appeals in a combat pilot association newsletter. "I was the one," it read.

Franz had moved to Canada in 1953 and became a successful businessman. A phone call confirmed everything; Charlie was finally able to thank him for saving his life and the lives of his crew that day. The two men did indeed meet, and became close friends for the rest of their days.

Chapter 5

An Answered Prayer

In times of desperation, people have often found inspiration and strength in the natural world around them. The legend of Robert the Bruce (King Robert I of Scotland), struggling to defeat the English in medieval times, took refuge in a cave where he noticed a spider. Several times the little creature tried to fix its thread to the walls of the cave, but on every attempt, the strand broke away, but it would not give up until, eventually, it succeeded and spun a beautiful web; its determination and resolve spurred the king to fight on and never give up - just like that spider.

During the Second World War, a different spider came to the aid of another young man, a young US marine, who had become separated from his unit on a Pacific Island during a battle against Japanese troops. The fighting had been fierce, and he found it impossible to find his way through the thick smoke and gunfire explosions.

Alone and unsure of what to do, he peered through the jungle trees, trying to work out where his comrades might have gone. Suddenly, he heard the sound of Japanese soldiers drawing near, and he made for cover. Scrambling through the thick foliage, he came to a ridge and several small caves beyond. With no time to lose, he clambered over it and into one of the caves. Once inside, he stopped and caught his breath.

Perhaps he had made a mistake; if the enemy soldiers made a search of the area, they would certainly find and kill him. As he waited, sweating, his heart in his mouth, he turned to prayer. "Lord, if it is your will, please protect me. Whatever your will, though, I love you, and I trust you. Amen."

Feeling a little calmer, he listened, and soon he heard the Japanese troops making a thorough search of the area. "Well," he thought, "I guess the Lord isn't going to help me out of this one." He lay there silently, not daring to move, wondering what would become of him.

At the entrance of the cave, he noticed a spider beginning to spin its web across the opening. "Ha! What I need is a stone wall, and what the Lord has sent me is a spider web. God certainly does have a sense of humor!"

He watched the spider painstakingly weaving its web, strand by strand, gradually spiraling and interlacing its gossamer threads. In just a few minutes, the diligent spider had methodically woven its web right across the entrance to the cave. Outside, the young marine's hunters had started to search the caves. Preparing himself for the worst, the young marine waited to be discovered.

But the soldiers passed by his cave. How could this be? He realized that when they came across that intricate web, they had quickly decided that anyone trying to enter that cave would have broken it with their body. It never occurred to them that this wonder of nature could have been created so quickly; they were confident that no one could have entered it that day.

"Lord, forgive me!" prayed the young man. "I had forgotten that in you, a spider's web is stronger than a stone wall!" He remained hidden until he was certain the Japanese had moved on, and once he was convinced all was clear, he scrambled out and went to find his comrades.

This story has been told before, in the Old Testament of the Bible. God, foreseeing that Saul would come to a cave where David and his men were sheltering, caused a spider to weave its web across the entrance convincing Saul that it would be useless to search since the web indicated nobody had entered. Similarly, an English Catholic priest, fearing he would be discovered during a period of persecution during the Reformation, hid away in a secret priest hole' in a stately home, and an intact web satisfied his pursuers that he couldn't be there. The same story is found in the Islamic tradition, when the Prophet and his companion, chased by their enemies, took refuge in the cave of Thawr.

The message, however, is the same. What might be perceived as weak and fragile could actually prove to be something of great strength and of vital importance in the right circumstances. Whenever everything seems hopeless, having faith and the power of prayer can be a great comfort and support that may provide the means to salvation.

Chapter 6

A Loving Reunion

In the Spring of 1944, Norwood Thomas was a twenty-one-year-old American soldier stationed in Britain, preparing for the invasion of France. One day, he was visiting Richmond in southwest London with his friend. While they were taking a leisurely stroll by the River Thames, they came across two pretty young women trying to hire a rowing boat and cheekily suggested they would be better off taking two boats, so they could couple up, then the girls could row them along the river.

Laughing, the girls agreed, and Joyce Durrant, aged just seventeen, found herself rowing the handsome young American, Norwood. It soon became clear that they liked each other very much. Norwood thought Joyce had "a smile that melts" and liked how Joyce called him 'Tommy.' They arranged to meet again and were soon seeing each other whenever they could in the weeks that followed. They enjoyed going for walks (when the weather was fine), going for dinner at their favorite café, late night movies at the cinema, and they even managed a few trips to seaside villages.

All too soon, Norwood was posted overseas. As a skilled paratrooper with the 101st Airborne Division, he was dropped in a field near Sainte-Mère-Église in Normandy on D-Day, 6 June 1944. He thought he would only be there for three days, but he was still in northern France, fighting on the frontline, six weeks later. He often thought of Joyce, and whenever he managed to slip back to Britain, they would get together for a date or two.

After the Battle of Normandy, the Allied forces progressed toward Germany. Norwood served in Operation Market Garden in September 1944, an attempt to seize key bridges in the Netherlands, and in the Battle of the Bulge, during which he injured his back and spent a few days in hospital when the jeep he was traveling in skidded off the road and upturned after being hit by artillery fire.

As his unit finally advanced into Germany, the men of the 101st Airborne helped at a recently liberated concentration camp, probably Dachau. Norwood was one of the men responsible for organizing the transport for some of the survivors needing medical care.

When Germany finally surrendered on 8 May 1945, Norwood was in the second wave of American service personnel to be sent home. He departed from Marseilles in France on the *USS Worcester Victory* with several souvenirs; his D-Day parachute, a Nazi flag he had taken from a building, some German money, and a Luger pistol he had taken from a German officer in France.

"Orders to go home came so quick that there was no real chance to say goodbye." He recalled, but when he arrived in Massachusetts fifteen days later (and more than two years after he had left his home country for Europe), he wasted no time in writing to Joyce back in England, suggesting she might join him in the United States.

Unfortunately, Joyce misunderstood something in Norwood's letter and thought he was writing to let her know that he had found someone else and was breaking off their relationship. In time, she married and moved to Australia while Norwood, who had found it hard to settle into civilian life after his wartime experiences, rejoined the army and continued his military service and fought in Korea and Vietnam. He also got married and had a family too.

After he had retired and his wife had passed away, Norwood often found his mind wandering about his time in Europe. On his ninetieth birthday, wanting to reconnect with those days, he made a tandem parachute jump that hit the local papers. He often talked fondly about his memories and, in particular, about

Joyce, his first love. He had always kept his photographs of her but believed she had been killed in an aircraft accident many years before.

Meanwhile, Joyce, in Australia, had an unhappy marriage that ended in divorce. She also liked to think about the past and imagine how different her life might have been if she had married her 'Tommy.' Her son wondered what had happened to her American sweetheart and, after searching online, found the news reports of Norwood's parachute jump.

She was able to contact Norwood's son, and soon the elderly couple were reunited, after seventy years, on an internet video call. "When she called me 'Tommy,' her nickname for me, oh my God! It stirred emotions that had been dormant a long time." Norwood said. Joyce felt just the same; it was wonderful to see him after all these years. After shedding a few happy tears, the years seemed to fall away as the pair reminisced about all the golden times they had shared in the spring of 1944. Neither had ever expected they would ever hear from one another again; it seemed like a miracle.

Reuniting on a small screen, with 10,000 miles between them, was all very well, but it just wasn't quite the same as meeting face to face. When a New Zealand airline heard about Joyce and Norwood, it couldn't resist coming to their rescue and made arrangements to fly him to Adelaide, Australia, and, in 2016, the elderly couple were finally together again, just in time for Valentine's Day.

At first, they found it difficult to find any words; they just held each other tightly. "This is about the most wonderful thing that could have happened to me," said Norwood once he had managed to find his voice. "Good!" smiled Joyce, "We're going to have a wonderful fortnight."

Chapter 7

The Spirit of Christmas

The Battle of the Bulge, or as many know it, the *Ardennes Offensive*, was Hitler's last major military campaign of the Second World War, and it ran from 16 December 1944 until 28 January 1945. By then, both sides were battle weary and hoped for a swift end to the hostilities.

Fritz Vincken was a young German boy aged twelve at that time. He and his mother had fled from their family home in Aachen two months earlier, when the city had been captured by American forces after nineteen days of bitter conflict. They had moved into a small cottage in the Hürtgen forest and lived there quietly until the tanks and guns rolled into the area. The Allies prepared to push ahead further into Germany while the Germans were ready to doggedly defend their nation.

As the Battle of the Bulge got underway, a series of bloody battles were fought in the Hürtgen forest in the days that led up to Christmas. It was a cold winter and a frightening time, Fritz recalled after the war, "We heard the incessant booming of field guns; planes soared continuously overhead; at night searchlights stabbed through the darkness."

On Christmas Eve, as Fritz and his mother were settling down for the evening, there was a knock at the door. When Frau Vincken opened it, she was surprised to find three American soldiers nervously standing there, one badly wounded. Unable to speak any English, and the servicemen unable to understand German, they managed to communicate in broken French, and she invited them inside the cottage and to make themselves comfortable.

"We learned that the stocky, dark-haired fellow was Jim; his friend, tall and slender, was Robin. Harry, the wounded one, was now sleeping on my bed, his face as white as the snow outside. They'd lost their battalion and had wandered in the forest for three days, looking for the Americans and hiding from the Germans. "They hadn't shaved, but still, without their heavy coats, they merely looked like big boys. And that was the way Mother began to treat them."

Fritz's mother started to prepare a meal of potatoes and the capon (chicken) that they had been saving for a celebratory dinner when Fritz's father returned from the war. As the soldiers began to relax in the warm kitchen, the first proper home they had experienced for many months, there was a second knock at the door.

"Expecting to find more lost Americans, I opened the door without hesitation," Fritz recalled. However, this was not the case. "There stood four soldiers, wearing the uniforms quite familiar to me after five years of war. They were *Wehrmacht* – Germans! I was frozen with fear. Although still a child, I knew the harsh law: sheltering enemy soldiers constituted high treason. We could all be shot!"

The Corporal in command of the small patrol spoke to Fritz's mother. He explained that they were lost and couldn't find their regiment in the dark and asked if they might stay and rest in her home until daylight the next morning.

"Of course," she replied, "You can share a fine, warm meal with us and eat until the pot is empty. But, we have three other guests staying tonight, whom you may not consider friends. But tonight is Christmas Eve, and there will be no shooting in this home."

The Corporal demanded, "Who is inside? *Amerikaner?*" Fritz's mother replied, "Listen to me. You could be my sons, just as these young men inside. There's a boy with a gunshot wound, fighting for his life, and his two friends are lost just like you and as hungry and exhausted as you are. This one night, this Christmas night, let us forget about war and killing."

The Germans came in and politely stacked their guns by the door. The Americans looked at one another in alarm. Quickly, Fritz's mother explained to them, in French, what she had said to the Germans, and they handed their weapons over to her. The men looked at one another uncomfortably, then sat down to share the meal.

AFTER A LITTLE WHILE, the soldiers began to feel more at ease. Fritz learned a little about them; Heinz and Willi, aged sixteen, were both from Cologne. The Corporal, at twenty-three, was the oldest. Even to Fritz, they all looked to be little more than schoolboys. From his pack, the Corporal took a bottle of red wine and put it on the table, and Heinz offered a small rye loaf from his bag. Frau Vincken carefully divided the bread between them all to eat with the dinner. She then shared the wine but left half in the bottle "for the wounded boy." As they all sat around the table, she recited the old German table prayer, "*Komm, Herr Jesu; sei du Unser Gast,*" (Come, Lord Jesus, be our guest). Fritz could see tears in his mother's eyes, and as he looked around the table, he saw that some of their guests had tears in their eyes too.

Just before midnight, Fritz's mother went to the doorstep and opened the door. She looked into the clear dark sky and beckoned to her guests, asking them to join her. Everyone, except Harry who was sleeping, peered into the heavens at the gleaming stars and searched for the brightest of them all, the Star of Bethlehem, in wondrous silence. It was a moment Fritz would never forget. Just for a moment, the war that had blighted all of their lives for so long was almost forgotten.

The next morning, the soldiers shook hands and departed in opposite directions, back to their battle lines.

While it is well known how some First World War soldiers shook hands across the trenches on Christmas Day and put aside their weapons, even enjoying a game of football in an area of no-man's-land in Belgium in 1914, there are very few known examples of enemies coming together at Christmas in the Second World War. Military commanders did not want their men fraternizing with the enemy they were fighting against, encouraging them to see the differences rather than common ground, but it is perfectly possible that Franz Vincken's little cottage was by no means the only one where enemies broke bread together, in the spirit of Christmas, during the Second World War.

Chapter 8

Music of the Night

The Battle of Stalingrad was one of the most brutal and bloodiest conflicts of modern warfare. It began on 23 August 1942 when the German *Luftwaffe* began to bomb the city. Hitler had publicly stated his intention to destroy Stalingrad, named after Joseph Stalin, the Soviet Union premier; he believed this would shatter Russian morale and allow him to take the valuable oil fields in that area.

The largest and most battle-hardened German troops quickly advanced into the city but soon found the Soviet Red Army was not on the verge of collapse as they had been told. After months of bitter street fighting in the ruins of Stalingrad, the German forces realized that they had been surrounded by their enemy. This meant it was almost impossible for them to receive ammunition, supplies, and food. As winter drew in, the weather deteriorated, and the invading army found themselves ill-prepared for the freezing winds and blizzards.

Despite receiving reports that his men were starving and suffering from frostbite and hypothermia in temperatures as low as -40° Celsius, Hitler would not allow them to surrender. Desperate and exhausted, all they could focus on was trying to survive.

As the situation for these German soldiers became increasingly hopeless, the Soviet forces breathed a sigh of relief in the knowledge that it was only a matter of time before they could declare victory. This would be Hitler's first major defeat and the turning point in the war, so there was much to celebrate. Over the festive period, senior Soviet officers held several parties and invited actors, musicians, and ballerinas to perform at an open-air concert for their troops.

One of the musicians was Mikhail Goldstein, a German composer, and violinist of Jewish descent. Born in Odesa, he became a naturalized Soviet citizen with the rest of his family in 1918 and had studied the violin since he was four years old.

When the concert had finished, the artists and performers were supposed to stay well away from the devastated war zones of Stalingrad, where the Soviet soldiers sheltered in their trenches, ready to defend the city against any desperate final onslaught the Germans might attempt, still exchanging gunfire from time to time. But, horrified at the state of the bomb-damaged, ruined city, Mikhail wanted to do more and went to these combat trenches to play for those on the front line.

Since Hitler had declared war on the Soviet Union, all German music had been banned by the Russian Government, but Mikhail thought to himself, "Tonight is New Year's Eve; they are hardly going to arrest me for playing some fine German music," and began to play some of what he considered to be the finest music ever composed for the violin, by the celebrated composer, Johann Sebastian Bach. The beautiful music, amplified by loudspeakers, cut through the silent winter night and soared in the air. All the shooting stopped; it was not just the Soviet soldiers who were listening to the melodies with rapt attention.

As he came to an end and prepared to leave, a voice from a loudspeaker from the German lines could be heard in broken Russian; it begged Mikhail to play some more Bach, "Please," it said, "We won't shoot...."

How could he refuse? He picked up his violin and, with a flourish of his bow, played a lively gavotte - a traditional folk dance - for both sides to enjoy. It's hard to imagine how those German soldiers must have felt; demoralized, filthy, and starving, unable to keep warm in the disheveled uniforms they had been wearing since the summer, tatty, broken boots, and little else to keep out the biting cold, unused to coping with the Russian winter. For a few minutes, they were spirited away from their misery by the exquisite music that would have been very familiar to so many of them; just a little while for them to rise above the dreadful conditions and the grim future that must have been of great concern to each of them; surrender and shame or death.

The Battle of Stalingrad formally ended on 2 February 1943. Overall, it is estimated that more than 1.2 million people lost their lives in that conflict which Hitler had believed would be an easy victory. Mikhail survived the war and often spoke of that night when he saw how music has the power to bring people together across great divides and comfort those in desperate need.

Chapter 9

A Sailor's Best Friend

Simon's town (or Simonstad), on the western cape of South Africa, is home to the country's largest naval bases and was a naval base for the British Royal Navy. In 1938, as the world was preparing for war, the naval authorities based at Simon's Town had an unusual little dilemma of their own to resolve.

The dilemma's name was *Just Nuisance*. He was a young Great Dane who belonged to Benjamin Chaney, in charge of the United Services Institute. Quite a character from the start, Just Nuisance became popular with the sailors, who liked to give him treats and take him for walks. He was an enormous dog, even for a Great Dane (almost two meters tall when standing on his back legs), and he became a familiar sight lolloping along next to his sailor friends.

Just as the high-spirited young men would get into trouble from time to time, so did Just Nuisance! He often accompanied them when they spent their shore leave having a few drinks and led them back to the base; unfortunately, he wasn't always capable of putting the right (drunken) sailor on the right ship, and it wasn't unusual for a sailor from another base to wake up, confused, at Simon's Town.

After a long walk, he would often curl up on the gangplank of one of the ships docked in the harbor. He found *HMS Neptune* particularly comfortable, but while he slept, no one could get past, and it is thought that this is where he picked up his name, 'Just Nuisance.'

The sailors made a fuss of their friend, who was always happy to walk with a young man wearing the distinctive bell-bottomed trousers he always seemed to recognize. On one occasion, in the nearby town of Fish Hoek, the sailors he was with had become rather too tipsy, and when a police officer decided their behavior had become too much and was busy writing down their names and details in his notebook, Just Nuisance took it, chewed it up, then chased him away to the delight of the drunken sailors, who were very relieved to have escaped arrest. The details of this escapade soon spread around the naval base and the town. Just Nuisance was becoming famous.

One problem arose when Just Nuisance started traveling by train with his pals. Dogs were strictly forbidden on this public transport, and whenever a conductor found him, even when he was in disguise (the sailors would sometimes dress him in their uniforms), he would be unceremoniously dumped at the next station. Undeterred, he would simply get on the next train - and hope the conductor on that carriage would not see him or be a bit more sympathetic and turn a blind eye.

Although most of the other passengers found these antics amusing and even offered to pay his fare, some did complain. The train company finally threatened to seize Just Nuisance and have him put to sleep if he continued.

This was unthinkable! Outrageous! The dog had become a local celebrity and a living legend for Royal Navy personnel; every young sailor passing through Simon's Town wanted to have a drink in the company of Just Nuisance - local cafés and bars even put a dog bowl out to encourage the dog so the young men would spend their money with them. The Great Dane became the unlikely subject of diplomatic cables between Cape Town and London.

The extraordinary solution was for Just Nuisance to be enlisted into the Royal Navy. He was given the rank of Ordinary Seaman on Friday, 25 August 1939, and since servicemen could travel free of charge on the railways, this would enable him to continue traveling exactly as he had before without any fear of being turfed off. His trade was listed as 'bone cruncher,' his religion 'scrounger,' and, like all recruits, he was given his own conduct papers. These are still held and exhibited at Simon's Town's local museum; the long list of misdemeanors recorded included going AWOL (absent without leave), losing his collar, sleeping in the petty officer's dormitory (for which he was punished, and had all bones removed for seven days) and, rather ironically, traveling on a train without his free pass. It also records him fighting with - and killing - some of the naval ship's mascots.

When an officer ordered the men to stand to attention, he would often find Just Nuisance at the end of the line, sitting up straight and ready for inspection, with his cap at a jaunty angle.

Although he never actually went to sea, he did his bit for the war effort; he 'married' another Great Dane called Adinda, and together, they had five gorgeous puppies that were auctioned off to raise funds. This might well have been the reason for his promotion soon afterward.

On 1 January 1944, after almost five years of service, Just Nuisance had to be discharged from service. He was suffering from thrombosis after a car accident. Sadly, his health quickly deteriorated until he could hardly walk and was in a great deal of pain. He was taken to the town's naval hospital, where the Naval Veterinary Officer felt he had no option but to put him to sleep on 1 April that same year. His body was draped with the White Ensign of the Royal Navy, and he was buried with full naval honors and a gun salute as the Last Post played. His grave, on the top of the hill at Klawer, the former South Africa Navy Signal School, is marked with a granite headstone.

Simon's town will never forget Just Nuisance. A bronze statue, complete with a collar and a Royal Navy cap, was unveiled in the town's Jubilee Square in 1985, and every year there is an annual parade for Great Danes with the dog that looks the most like Just Nuisance awarded a prize.

There are some in South Africa who feel uncomfortable about all the privileges that were given to the dog; at that time, most non-white people were desperately poor and subjected to segregation; they were not allowed to travel on some of the train carriages that he traveled in, or to visit many of the bars and cafés. But, of course, Just Nuisance never asked for any special treatment; he was just happy to be a good friend doing what dogs have done for centuries - providing comfort, companionship, entertainment, and instinctively knowing how to brighten everyone's day.

Chapter 10

Moral Victory

The end of the Second World War in Europe and the final fall of Hitler's Third Reich was ultimately decided at the Battle of Berlin - which devastated the city from the 16th of April to the 2nd of May 1945.

The Soviet Red Army had relentlessly advanced on Germany, having defeated Hitler's armies in Poland, then Hungary. On the 30th of March 1945, they entered Austria and, within two weeks, had captured Vienna. The USAAF (US Army Air Force) launched a massive daylight bombing campaign on the German capital, and for 36 nights in succession, squadrons of British bombers played their part. By the 11th of April, American forces were just 100km (62 miles) from Berlin.

On the 20th of April, Hitler's birthday, the Soviets began shelling Berlin. The once proud city was in ruins. The civilians left there were traumatized and desperate, with no one left to defend them other than remnants of disorganized, recently defeated units of the German Army, along with civilian volunteers and the Hitler Youth to try and fight against the might of the Red Army while the German High Command retreated to Hitler's bunker.

In February 1945, General *Walther Wenck* was in charge of what was to be the last German armored battle on the Eastern Front. In Pomerania, his Army attempted to fight off the advancing Soviet Union troops. Hitler had given orders that General Wenck was to drive all the way from the battlefield to Berlin and to report to him in person every day. During one of those trips, he fell asleep at his wheel and crashed his car. General Wenck was badly hurt and spent several weeks in hospital, but before he could make a full recovery, Hitler named him Commander of his new 12th Army.

General Wenck, wearing a surgical corset due to several broken ribs that hadn't yet healed and in a great deal of discomfort, arrived at the 12th Army headquarters and soon found that it was not the organized, well-equipped fighting force he had hoped for; this new Army had just a few tanks and armored cars, some artillery guns and nowhere near the 100,000 men he had expected to command; there was barely 55,000 - most of whom were young cadets, elderly men, training officers with little battle experience, wounded soldiers who had not yet recovered and a large group of children, still at school, from the Hitler Youth. His orders were to fight against the American advance from the west, and once his troops had crossed the River Elbe, they prepared to make a stand, but then he received new orders.

On the 23rd of April, while the Red Army were encircling Berlin, the Chief of German Armed Forces, General Staff Field Marshal *Keitel*, drove to see General Wenck at his command post and ordered him to prepare an immediate attack towards Berlin in order to "save the Führer." After the war, the General said he couldn't recall Keitel making any mention of the millions of desperate civilians stranded in the capital; his priority and only concern was saving Hitler. He said General Wenck was the Führer's last hope.

General Wenck was dismayed and appalled at his senior officer's disregard for the German people, most of them defenseless, but did not protest, knowing he would be relieved of his command. Instead, he agreed to follow Keitel's orders and told his men, "Boys, you've got to go in once more," so his 12th Army, with few vehicles and almost no fuel, advanced towards the west of Berlin, most of them on foot. When they neared Potsdam, a city on the border of Berlin, it became clear that the Red Army had completely encircled Berlin, and the forces and civilians that remained inside the city were cut off. It was then that General Wenck realized all he could do was to try and help them; he made up his mind to concentrate on getting as many people away from the Soviet advance as possible and ordered his men to make an attack northeastwards, towards the city, where another German army had been surrounded, to create a corridor to Berlin through which those stranded in the city could flee.

In the early morning hours of the 26th of April, General Wenck's 12th Army made what was to be the final German offensive of the war and drove into the Soviet positions with their artillery guns. They caught the Soviets by surprise and managed to push forward. They went for days without sleep and had hardly any food to sustain them, and were under constant attack from the enemy; they suffered many casualties. As they approached the outskirts of Berlin, hundreds of civilians and bedraggled, limping soldiers of the 9th Army that had almost been destroyed, joined them.

The shelling continued as they progressed, but for twenty-four hours, they managed to hold off the enemy while they got hundreds of nurses, Red Cross workers, and wounded soldiers out of a large military hospital.

On the 2nd of May, General Wenck's Army retreated. Protecting the refugees they had rescued, his soldiers brought them across the River Elbe and into the hands of the American forces - It is believed that he helped as many as 250,000 refugees flee from the fall of Berlin and the dreadful treatment the Red Army subjected the German people to when they broke into the city. The Western Allies were a far better prospect for the defeated Germans, more sympathetic and bound by humanitarian conventions to show mercy than the brutal and vengeful Soviets. General Wenck was amongst the last to cross the river. He remained a prisoner of war until his release in 1947.

It is difficult to understand the frantic confusion and fear in Berlin during the last stages of the war. The city was devastated, much of it reduced to rubble from endless air raids; the civilians within the city were well aware that the enemy was closing in, but Hitler would not allow surrender; he expected his people to fight to the last while he remained cocooned in his bunker. General Wenck was horrified at the state of the people that his commanders expected to defend the city against close to a million Soviet soldiers.

By conducting his rescue mission, he failed to obey orders and went against the wishes of his Führer, to whom he had sworn loyalty. He was prepared to do the right thing by his people, and it is fitting that the last German offensive by men wearing Nazi uniforms was for humanitarian aid rather than the abhorrent ideals and objectives that will forever be associated with Germany in the Second World War.

Chapter 11

The City of Forgiveness

On the 8th of December 1941, the United States of America declared war on Japan. The Japanese surprise attack against the naval base on Pearl Harbor shocked the American public and forced their country into a war that had seemed, to many, a long way from their shores.

In the months and years that followed, American forces played a pivotal role in the Allied victory in Europe and then in the Far East and, despite fears that the United States would suffer the same bombing raids that had devastated other parts of the world, it remained almost entirely free from aerial attacks.

In retaliation for the strike on Pearl Harbor, in April 1942, the USAF (US Air Force) mounted a major bombing attack on Tokyo and other Japanese cities, known as the *Doolittle Raid*. Although it did not inflict a great deal of damage, it boosted morale on the

American home front and embarrassed the Japanese Navy, that had to answer for the presence of an enemy aircraft carrier able to launch bombers so close to the Japanese Home Islands.

One Japanese naval pilot, who was supposed to serve in the attack on Pearl Harbor, had his seaplane suffer technical difficulties. He swore revenge on America for the Doolittle Raid; his name was Nobuo Fujita.

He had also been present at the attempted shelling of the Fort Stevens US base near Astoria, Oregon, and believed he had a better idea for an assault. He suggested an aircraft loaded with bombs could be launched from a submarine situated near the Pacific coast of America in order to attack strategic targets on the US, and in particular, the Panama Canal. This idea interested the Imperial Navy's high command, and Nobuo was posted back to his long-range submarine aircraft carrier, I-25, to attempt such a raid.

At 06h00 on the 9th of September 1942, the submarine surfaced near the Oregon-California border. The submarine technicians prepared his wheelless Yokosuka E14Y "Glen" seaplane, loaded it with two incendiary bombs weighing 154kg (340lb), and readied the catapult required for its take-off. Nobuo and Petty Officer Okuda Shoji began their flight; it was to be the first aerial bombing raid on the continental United States.

Nobuo's target was Oregon. His bombs were to be dropped on dense forest areas in the hope they would start huge fires that would spread to towns and settlements and would need lots of resources to extinguish them; resources that were being used as part of the American coastal defenses, guarding the country against Japanese warships and submarines. Nobuo was a bit disappointed; he had dreamed of causing devastation in Los Angeles or San Francisco.

The Glen flew over Oregon at a speed of 90 mph and dropped the two bombs over remote forestland, the first on Wheeler Ridge on Mount Emily started a small fire that was easily contained, and the other was never found; the raid had come to nothing. Recent rains had left the ground damp, so fires were never going to take hold. The four US Forest Service staff who attended the Mount Emily fire found 27kg (60lbs) of bomb fragments and handed them over to the Army.

Despite foggy weather, the little plane was spotted by several people, especially when it flew over the city of Brookings. With its mission complete, it came down next to the submarine and into the ocean, and the submarine mechanics used a crane to pick it out of the water.

Lookouts reported the enemy assault, and USAAF patrols found and shot at the submarine - but it dived beneath the waves and escaped without much damage.

Three weeks later, on the 29th of September, Nobuo set out for another raid in his Glen, but it was equally as ineffective as his earlier mission. Soon afterward, the I-25 moved on, torpedoing and sinking two tanker ships as it left the Oregon coast, *SS Camden* (killing one crew member) on the 4th of October and the *SS Larry Doheny* (killing six of her crew) on the 5th of October, as it moved back into Japanese waters.

After the war, Nobuo, like most people caught up in the Second World War, tried to put his experiences behind him. He married and settled in the Ibaraki prefecture of Japan and opened a hardware store, and then worked in the manufacturing industry.

In 1962, the Brookings Junior Chamber of Commerce (an American organization) proposed inviting Nobuo Fujita to be an honorary guest at the annual Azalea Festival in a gesture of goodwill. Although there were some objections, most of the community supported the idea, happy to move on from wartime prejudices.

Nobuo had also been thinking about his experiences and was finding it increasingly difficult to come to terms with his point of view and his country's position during the war. He decided to accept the invitation from Brookings to try and make amends (once the Japanese government had been assured that he wouldn't be arrested and tried for war crimes).

The people of Brookings gave Nobuo and his family the warmest welcome. He had been concerned that he might have been pelted with rotten eggs or shouted at in the street, but he needn't have worried. The McChesney family, who had been involved in the scheme from the start, had opened their home to the Japanese guests, and the families developed a close friendship. One morning, Nobuo showed Bill McChesney his family's most prized possession, a samurai sword that had been handed through their generations for 400 years. Nobuo had taken it on every flight he had made, including the bombing missions over Brookings. He confessed that he had intended to use it for *seppuku*, a Japanese suicide ritual, if the people of Brookings confronted him about his war actions in 1942 and the disgrace became too much for him to bear. Rather than keeping it in his family, he presented the sword to the city that had shown him such forgiveness, courtesy, and understanding.

For the rest of his life, Nobuo continued his friendship with the Americans and even sponsored a student exchange program. In 1992, he planted a tree at Wheeler Ridge, where one of his bombs had landed, as a gesture of peace, and five years later, just before his death, he was made an honorary citizen of Brookings, South Dakota.

Chapter 12

Judy

In 1943, in the midst of the Second World War, The Dickin Medal was unveiled in Britain to honor animals that carried out remarkable acts of courage in desperate times. The medallion, made of bronze, bears the words *'For Gallantry'* and *'We also serve'* in the center of an embossed laurel leaf and is mounted on a striped green, brown, and light blue ribbon representing water, earth, and the air - i.e., the naval, army and air force military services. One Dickin Medal, awarded in 1943, bears the following on its reverse; *'For magnificent courage and endurance in Japanese prison camps, which helped to maintain morale among her fellow prisoners - and also for saving many lives through her intelligence and watchfulness.'* The recipient of that medal was an English pedigree pointer dog, named Judy.

Judy was one of seven puppies born in a boarding kennel in Shanghai in the summer of 1936. That autumn, the crew of the river gunboat *HMS Gnat* bought her as the ship's mascot, and she was soon a familiar site on the Yangtze River. In 1938, another pointer mascot, Paul, on board a French gunboat caught her eye, and their friendship resulted in thirteen puppies that were given to various naval ships in the area.

In 1939, Judy was transferred to *HMS Grasshopper*, another gunboat, and for the first time, she set out to sea. Poor Judy was not a natural sailor and suffered badly from seasickness, but the crew looked after her, and by the time they reached their destination, Singapore, she had recovered.

The first stages of the Second World War passed by quietly for Judy, but the quietness was not to last. The Japanese Imperial Army captured Singapore, with fighting lasting from 8 to the 15th of February 1942. *HMS Grasshopper* was one of the last ships to depart, loaded with service personnel and civilians, making their escape. The ship set sail for Batavia in the Dutch East Indies, hoping to hide there, away from the attention of the Japanese Navy. Judy welcomed everyone aboard and enjoyed the fuss they made of her, but on the 14th of February, she barked a warning to the crew - Japanese aircraft were approaching. The ship's gunners tried to put up a fight, but the *Grasshopper* was hit by several bombs, and the captain gave the order to abandon the ship.

Lifeboats were hastily lowered, and the crew and evacuees were ferried to the nearest shore while the Japanese fighter planes fired their machine guns at them. When all were ashore and the enemy had gone, they found they were on an uninhabited island with no fresh water, and there was no sign of Judy. Once they had made a shelter, some of the crew went back to the wreckage of the *Grasshopper* to try and find any supplies that were still intact. There, they found her hiding in her bed under some lockers, but she was soon with everyone else on dry land and made herself useful; she protected everyone from snakes, and when the lack of water became a serious problem, Judy began to dig and found a freshwater spring.

Five days later, a *Chinese junk* (ship) arrived, and Judy found herself bound for Sumatra with the others. On arrival, they embarked on a grueling 200-mile trek along the northeast coast to Pedang, and, just a few miles from safety; they walked into an enemy-held village. Judy, hidden under some empty rice sacks, and the exhausted servicemen were trucked to Gloegoer Prisoner of War Camp in Medan.

At the camp, Judy met Leading Aircraftsman Frank Williams, and the two of them developed an extraordinary bond. As soon as he saw her, Frank wondered what such a beautiful dog could be doing there. Although she was very thin, he could see she was a survivor and began to share his meager daily rations with her; she adored him. She made herself useful, letting him and his friends know when there was danger; snakes, scorpions, or Japanese guards; anyone ready to beat one of her prisoner friends risked an encounter with a growling, snarling Judy, even though they fought her off with a kick or a blow with a rifle butt.

Frank was worried that she might go too far one day, so when the Camp Commandant was in a good mood (after a few glasses of sake), he talked him into registering Judy as a prisoner of war in exchange for any puppies she might have.

Although she was officially Prisoner 81A Gloergoer, Medan, this was no guarantee of her safety. In June 1944, Frank was transferred to Singapore aboard the *SS Van Warwyke* with more than 700 other men. The conditions on the ship were dreadful, the prisoners were forced to stand to attention on the ship's deck for hours in blistering heat, and Judy - unknown to the Japanese crew who would never have allowed a dog on the ship - had been trained to remain completely still and silent inside a rice sack, and remained slung over Frank's shoulder throughout.

The *Van Warwyke* was torpedoed. Frantically trying to save Judy, Frank pushed her through a porthole, and she landed in the water below. Then, he managed to get himself to safety. He was recaptured and taken to a new camp, but he had no idea what might have happened to his canine friend.

But, just as he thought he would never see her again, she turned up at the camp! She had been a true hero helping the ship's survivors to shore, letting them hang onto her as she swam through the dark, oily waters and guiding them towards floating debris, swimming to and from the shore until all the men were safe.

Frank and Judy were delighted to be together, but the new camp in Sumatra was the worst yet. There, the men were put to work building a railway, which was backbreaking work in tropical heat for several hours a day in exchange for tiny rations - a handful of maggoty, dirty rice. Frank gladly shared his with Judy, but the new guards, much more brutal and crueler than in the previous camp, soon grew tired of the now scraggy dog, snarling and snapping at them when they shouted their orders at the prisoners and threatened to kill her.

Frank felt sure they were serious and encouraged her to hide in the jungle. Ever resourceful and brave, she survived encounters with Sumatran tigers, crocodiles, and venomous snakes until finally, in August 1945, the guards left, and Judy came back to the camp as the men were liberated.

The troopship that brought the former prisoners back to Britain did not allow dogs, so once again, Judy had to be smuggled aboard. Once Frank had brought her home and her remarkable story became known, she was awarded her Dickin Medal. Frank took Judy to visit some of the grieving families of men that had died out in the camps, so far away, and she instinctively seemed to know exactly how to comfort them.

"Every day I thanked God for Judy," said Frank, "She saved my life in so many ways. The greatest way of all was giving me a reason to live. All I had to do was look at her and into those weary, bloodshot eyes, and I would ask myself, what would happen to her if I died? I had to keep going. Even if it meant waiting for a miracle."

Chapter 13

The Sugihara Visas

From the very beginning of his career, Adolf Hitler had two ambitions for Germany; to conquer huge swathes of Europe for his people to live in and to rid the world of Jews. While he was building the military and preparing for war, he was also building an appalling propaganda campaign against the Jewish people, and, from 1933, Nazi Germany introduced laws to restrict the rights of Jews. During the Second World War, the treatment of the German Jewish people worsened; they were persecuted and deported to concentration camps until 1942, resulting in their mass murder. The countries which Hitler had invaded, such as Poland, the Netherlands, and Czechoslovakia, were expected to contribute to this inhumane and barbaric program - and the other *Axis* countries that had aligned with Nazi Germany (Italy, Hungary, Romania, Bulgaria, Slovakia, and

Croatia) participated to some degree with the notable exception of Japan.

The people of Japan rarely held anti-Semitic views in the first half of the 20th Century. By declaring war on the United States of America and joining forces with the Axis countries, it was fighting to establish a Southeast Asian Empire; with Japan absorbing a bloc of countries in its vicinity, some European-owned territories, as well as Manchuria and Korea, rich in oil, rubber, and rice. For Japan, The Second World War was more about economics, land, and trade.

In the lead-up to the war, the attitude towards the Jews was not at the forefront of Japan's negotiations and agreements with Nazi Germany. Japan viewed anti-Semitism as a European issue, and Hitler did not press Japan into adopting his evil ideology.

One Japanese diplomat, Chiune Sugihara, vice-consul for the Imperial Japanese Empire in Kaunas, Lithuania, did not dismiss anti-Semiticism as simply a European issue and helped thousands of Polish and Lithuanian Jews escape the Holocaust.

Known as *'Sempo,'* Chiune Sugihara spoke fluent Russian and had been sent to Kaunas to report on German and Soviet troop movements, but as the war progressed, all diplomats were ordered to leave the country in 1940 as the Soviet Union, then aligned to Nazi Germany, began its occupation. Many Polish-Jewish families had fled to Lithuania after the invasion of Poland in 1939 but soon realized they were not safe and needed to leave urgently, but they could not cross the border without a visa which was virtually impossible to obtain from the Lithuanian authorities.

When desperate refugees went to Sempo, asking for a visa so they could travel through Japanese territory, he did not hesitate and gave them transit visas that allowed them to travel, by train, across Siberia, and to Japan. They could not know that he was going against his orders; when he had asked his superiors in Tokyo what he should do, he had been told not to issue documents to help the Jews.

However, he was prepared to issue visas to people who had no identity papers, members of youth groups, and students; the young people studying at the Mir Yeshiva center were able to leave Lithuania and spend the remainder of the war in a slum for 'stateless' people in Shanghai, under Japanese occupation, and certainly wouldn't have survived if they had remained in Europe.

Throughout July 1940, he spent long days issuing as many visas as he could, and even at Kaunas Railway Station as he prepared to leave, he was still writing them. There are witnesses who recalled seeing him throwing visas and blank sheets of paper, signed by him and stamped with the consulate seal (so the refugees could fill them in themselves), out of the carriage window and onto the platform after he had boarded the train. As he finally left, he bowed deeply to the people gathered at the station and said, "Please forgive me. I cannot write any more. I wish you the best."

"He did not care if they were citizens of the Netherlands, Poland, Germany, or Lithuania," said Nathan Lewin, who was three years old when his mother managed to get a 'Sugihara visa.' "He just saw them as human beings who needed to be rescued and whose lives were at stake."

Most of the refugees with visas traveled to Vladivostok and then to the Jewish community in Kobe in Japan, and, before the Japanese forces attacked Pearl Harbor, the Polish ambassador in Tokyo managed to get passages for some to go to Canada, New Zealand, the United States, and South America.

Sempo continued his diplomatic career, serving in Prague and then Romania. No one ever confronted him about the visas he had issued, although he always expected someone to ask him about the huge number of exit documents that bore his signature.

After the war, Sempo and his family remained in Europe as prisoners of war until 1947, when they were allowed to return to Japan. There, he was disciplined for disobeying his orders while he was in Lithuania and left the Japanese Foreign Office.

His actions were not forgotten. In 1985, *Yad Vashem*, Israel's official Holocaust memorial, honored Chiune Sugihara and declared him one of the 'Righteous Among the Nations.' Although he only issued around 2,000 visas, most were for families, so it is estimated that around 6,000 Jewish people survived the war due to Sempo, and more than 100,000 people alive today are estimated to have descended from those Jews. When he was asked why he did it, he said, "It is the kind of sentiment anyone would have when he or she actually sees refugees face to face, begging with tears in their eyes. He just cannot help but sympathize... I knew that somebody would surely complain about me in the future. But, I myself thought this would be the right thing to do."

Chapter 14

Night Flight

From the 10th of July to the 31st of October 1940 took place the *Battle of Britain* - the first major military campaign to be fought entirely by air forces. It raged over the southern counties of England. British fighter pilots of the RAF (Royal Air Force) took on the might of the *Luftwaffe* (the German Air Force), doggedly defending their country against large-scale attacks designed to weaken the country that was Hitler's next target for invasion.

Jack Adams had joined the RAF in 1936 and was a fully trained pilot when he was posted to 29 Squadron as acting Flight Lieutenant. This was a night fighter squadron of Bristol Blenheims, twin-engine high-performance light bombers.

One night in August 1940, Jack was on patrol, flying his Blenheim about a mile from his base at Gosport in Hampshire, when, in the night skies, he spotted the taillight of an enemy aircraft. For a second, he wondered what it could be doing alone in British airspace. Was it a trap?

Decisively, Jack made chase. Through the inky darkness, he closed in on the German plane with little thought for his own safety. For fifty minutes, he hunted it down, using the taillight to keep it in sight. Even when he lost radio contact and knew he was short of fuel, he continued, skillfully navigating through the skies.

Eventually, he closed in on his enemy and shot it down over the sea near the Isle of Wight. Only then did he bring his Blenheim back to the airfield. The ground crew there were completely astonished to find he was completely out of fuel.

Jack was awarded the Distinguished Flying Cross (DFC) for his selfless bravery and determination that night. The citation for this award stated that he had been "...*continuously employed on night duties*" since he had joined the squadron and had always demonstrated "*conspicuous devotion to duty.*"

Jack retired from the RAF in 1958, and by then, he held the rank of Wing Commander. His extraordinary night flight of August 1940 is remembered as an inspiring story of courage at a time when Britain was under real threat.

Chapter 15

The Parachute

Howard Linn, a young man from Radcliffe, Iowa, joined the USAAF (United States Army Air Force) during the Second World War. After his training, he became a waist gunner and aircraft engineer on a B-24J Liberator heavy bomber nicknamed the 'Silver Lady.'

He and the crew of the Silver Lady were assigned to the 859th Squadron of the 492nd Bomb Group with the 2nd Air Division of the US Eighth Air Force. Their first mission, on the 11th of May 1944, was to attack the oil refinery at Zeitz near Leipzig in Germany, and, on the 19th of May, they were to be part of a twenty-six-bomber raid on munition plants and a marshaling yard in the German city of Brunswick.

It was a miserable, overcast day, and after take-off, the bombers formed up and climbed high above the clouds. As they flew over German-occupied Europe, the group changed course and altitude from time to time, a technique that made it more difficult for enemy fighter planes to target them. But still, those enemy fighters soon arrived and set to work attacking the Allied fighters, escorting the formation and the bombers themselves. By the time they neared Brunswick, the air was thick with black smoke, and Howard could see fires caused by the falling bombs on the ground below. The Silver Lady dropped hers, and they began to turn back.

Then, a large group of Focke-Wulf 190 German fighters flew over the Silver Lady, "12 o'clock high," said Howard, turned around, and launched a head-on attack. Howard fired a few rounds from his machine gun, but the fighters were so fast, "like a streak," recalled Howard afterward. The No. 3 engine on the right wing was hit, and once the crew had managed to extinguish those flames, Howard noticed fire coming from the edge of the wing. He radioed the pilot, who asked if Howard could get at it with a fire extinguisher, but that was impossible. Moments later, burning hot air rushed into the aft compartment (the section by the aircraft tail where Howard was positioned with his waist gun), and Howard told the pilot he was going to bail out.

He tore off his microphone and oxygen mask, grabbed his parachute, and snapped it to his flying suit harness. He then opened the door at the base of the aircraft and dived out. Howard hoped the rest of the crew had got out as the Silver Lady exploded and seemed to disintegrate as he fell.

Howard lay on his back, spinning wildly, as he plummeted 20,000 feet to the ground, looking over his shoulder. He had never made a practice jump, "they told us our first jump has to be good anyway, so no need to practice." He remembered his instructors had told him not to open the parachute too early because it would take him longer to land - and easier to be spotted by the enemy leaving him little chance to avoid capture. He hurtled through thick clouds and finally pulled his ripcord when he could see trees that seemed to be hurtling towards him. The parachute opened with a jolt.

Landing safely in a clearing, Howard scrambled to his feet, pulled off the parachute and harness, then ran about half a mile into a forest. Only then did he realize he had forgotten to carry his army shoes. He had left them tied to his harness; his distinctive USAAF flying boots would give him away if he were captured, and this was a worry; he had heard about American airmen being caught by the inhabitants of bombed cities so angry about the devastation caused that they had beaten and tortured those airmen; or worse.

Once he was well away from where he had landed, he crawled under a large brush pile and opened his escape kit - concentrated chocolate, basic medical equipment, a compass, and maps printed onto silk, but as he had no idea where he was, the maps were of no use to him at that point. Sometimes he heard voices, probably patrols out looking for him having found the parachute, he decided. After dark, he moved deeper into the forest. "What is amazing, I actually did sleep part of the night, even though, being all alone in enemy country, I could have been killed by anyone coming along," said Howard.

The next morning he discarded his helmet and his flying suit, apart from the inner lining, and then using the compass, he made his way westward but remained near the wooded areas as much as he could. When he saw some windmills in the distance, he wondered whether he had been fortunate enough to have landed in the Netherlands or Belgium, where locals might be prepared to hide him from the Germans and help him to get back to Britain. Around midday, he came across a small village and decided to take a risk; he walked along the main road, smoking a cigarette in an attempt to blend in, and nodded to the people he passed.

A boy, aged around fifteen, saw Howard and recognized his flying boots. He spoke a little English, so Howard asked him if he was in the Netherlands. The boy told him he was in Rodewald, very much in Germany, and took him to his home, where his mother and Grandmother made him sandwiches and coffee. After some discussion, the German family decided they would have to hand Howard over to the authorities.

The boy flagged down a German police officer on a motorcycle, and he arranged for Howard to be picked up. "That's it. I was captured," he said. The next morning, he, along with two other captured Allied airmen, were taken to an interrogation center in Frankfurt. All his personal possessions, his ring, watch, penknife, and nail clippers, were confiscated, and he was placed in a cold, damp cell. He was questioned but only revealed his name, rank, and service number.

Howard and the other prisoners were packed into a railway carriage and traveled to Stettin and, from there, were marched for twenty miles to Stalag Luft IV. This POW (prisoner of war) camp was huge; at its largest, there were 7,089 American and 886 prisoners of other nationalities held there. It was surrounded by barbed wire fences and guarded by sentries with rifles who took their duties very seriously. The conditions were appalling; it was very cold, and there was no heating in the huts, there were no proper washing facilities or medical care, and the supplies of food were hardly enough for all the prisoners.

Early on the 5th of February 1945, the inmates of the camp were told to get their possessions and to help themselves to clothes and supplies from a store of Red Cross parcels as they would be leaving. Carrying as much as they could, Howard was one of the thousands of POWs that set off the following day in the cold winter winds, marching westwards.

They walked for 87 days, escorted by armed guards with dogs. They slept in barns or out in the open, sharing blankets, and were given very little food; what they did receive was often rotten and full of maggots. There was nowhere to wash, and most of the men were covered with lice that they had picked up in the dirty straw they slept on. Many became sick and did not survive. Howard said, "When we left Stalag Luft IV, there were 2,000 prisoners in my group, but by the time we got to an international Red Cross camp near Hanover, Germany, there were only 1,500 left." By then, they had been marching for 52 days.

They didn't stay at the Hanover camp for long. The British Army was rapidly advancing toward the area, so the prisoners set out again, passing through cities so bombed that they were little more than rubble. Over the days, the guards began to disappear, and 35 days later, British soldiers liberated the exhausted POWs. The War in Europe was over, and Howard was able to return home.

Back in Iowa, he met and married Betty and, eventually, bought his own farm. They completed their family with three daughters and a son. Howard reflected on his experiences; "I never worried if I was going to survive. I don't know why. All I can say is the Lord has been very good to me."

In 1994, Russell Ives, a Second World War researcher and the grandson of a man who served in the same

Bomber Group as Howard, got in touch. Howard told him all about his experiences and, through Russell, Wilfred Beerman, the youth he had met in the village of Rodewald, contacted him.

Wilfred still lived in the same house where Howard had been given sandwiches and coffee. He had always felt a heavy burden of guilt because his family had been unable to help Howard and had handed him over to the German authorities and felt very relieved that he had survived.

Despite all those grueling months in captivity, Howard said he had no reason to feel that way; "It was war," he said when they met in Germany,

"I forgive you."

Chapter 16

Good Gruber

Steve Richardson was born in December 1954, exactly ten years after his father had been fighting for his life in an enemy army field hospital, more than 4,000 miles from their home in Iowa.

Steve's father, *Elmer Richardson*, was working as a truck driver when young American men were first drafted to join the military services and fight against the Axis powers (at that time, Germany, Italy, and Japan) in the Second World War.

As experienced truck drivers were needed in the United States to drive supplies, Elmer was not part of that first draft, but as the war progressed and the military needed every man they could get (with women often taking on those essential jobs left vacant), in 1944 he was called up into the Army. He was inducted at Camp Dodge in Johnston, Iowa, then received his basic training at Tyler, Texas, before boarding a troopship in New York and sailing across the Atlantic to England.

Elmer was attached to the 12th Infantry, 4th Division and, having spent two years of the war driving his truck and helping the American war effort stateside, found he was a bit older and more mature than most of the others in his unit and the natural choice was for the Army to promote him to the rank of Sergeant. So they did.

In December 1944, Elmer's unit were in the Ardennes, an ancient forest that extends over the north of Luxembourg, southeast of Belgium, and northwest France. It was there that the Germans made their last major offensive to try and push the Allied forces back and prevent them from entering Germany.

On the 18th of December, two days after the battle had begun, Elmer was out in a jeep with another sergeant, patrolling an area of the Hürtgen Forest near the Belgian German border, when they ran into a German ambush. The enemy soldiers shot at Elmer, and his jeep ran into a deep ditch at the roadside. Despite suffering gunshot wounds to his abdomen, Elmer managed to evade capture for a while but on the 20th of December, he was picked up by a German patrol and taken to a field hospital at Helenenberg Abbey.

Elmer's wounds were grave and needed immediate attention. A German army medic, Ludwig Gruber, realized he would not survive without surgery and got to work operating on him. Dr. Gruber had completed his medical training in 1938 and had been drafted into the *Wehrmacht* (German Army) in 1940. He had been posted to Russia, and there he had treated countless casualties with war wounds as well as men suffering from the effects of dreadful conditions; many German troops were starving and frozen in the brutal Soviet winter. "Hundreds and hundreds of soldiers must have been on Dr. Gruber's operating table," Elmer's son, Steve, said.

During surgery, Dr. Gruber could see that the bullet had penetrated Elmer's bowels, cut into his liver, and damaged other organs. He spent hours working on his patient, using new techniques to repair the bowel and save his life. The officers in charge of the field hospital were unhappy with him spending so much time and effort to save one of the enemies, especially when there were injured German soldiers that needed his help, and told him to stop, but the doctor refused. He completed the operation, and it was a success; Elmer survived.

Dr. Gruber took a great interest in his recovery and fought to stop the *Wehrmacht* from taking him to a prisoner-of-war camp until he was satisfied his American patient was well enough to leave. He wrote his address in Germany on a bit of paper and asked Elmer to write to him after the war.

In the extra week that Elmer stayed at Helenenberg Hospital, a US Army captain visited under a truce, and while he was there, he spoke to him. He revealed that there were plans to bomb that area because German military vehicles and artillery guns were being held there. Elmer and the captain managed to negotiate with the officers in command, and it was agreed that if the vehicles were moved, the Americans would abandon their plans and leave the hospital unscathed. This deal would save many lives.

After the war, Elmer, still recovering from his wounds, was repatriated to a military hospital in Iowa. The surgeons there were very impressed at Dr. Gruber's expertise and took a special interest in the procedures he had used. Elmer wrote to him and thanked him for his care and kindness, and Dr. Gruber wrote back, delighted that his American patient had survived the war.

Elmer went back to driving his truck and, in his later years, drove a school bus. He rarely spoke about his wartime experiences in Europe, even though Steve often asked. After his death in 1996, Steve and his wife decided to go to Belgium and Germany to try and retrace Elmer's war using his unit's daily battle reports that are held at the National Archives, information from the World War 2 museum in New Orleans, and documents that Elmer had kept. The expedition was a great success; Steve felt sure he had worked out exactly where his father had been.

He had tried to trace Dr. Gruber online but, since Gruber is a very common German name, he didn't hold much hope of finding him but; while they were in Germany, the Richardsons received an email from one of Dr. Gruber's sons. Ludwig Gruber had passed away, but his three sons, two of whom were doctors like him, were eager to meet with Steve and hear about Elmer.

"I felt like I gained three brothers," said Steve afterward. The men talked for nine hours, discussing their late fathers and wondering why Dr. Gruber had chosen to help Elmer against his orders, probably risking his career and good name with the *Wehrmacht*. Perhaps it was simply that even at a time of hatred and war, the doctor simply saw his patients as fellow men, whatever uniform they were wearing, and his duty was to treat and heal them.

Chapter 17

The Volksdeutsche

After Hitler's forces had swept through Europe, many of the people of those countries were unhappy with the Nazi regime imposed upon them and longed for the day they would be liberated. Most believed they had to make the best of a bad situation, but some very brave men and women could not accept it and needed to do something more. They created small groups to help the Allies and operated in strict secrecy, whether committing acts of sabotage to cause difficulties for the Germans or gathering information and sending reports that might be of use to the British and American war offices.

The resistance also arranged 'evasion and escape lines.' This was a system by which downed Allied airmen were located, then fed, clothed, given forged identity documents, then hidden in people's homes, cellars, attics, and outbuildings by a network of volunteers. These evaders were also accompanied by Resistors who guided them as they moved along the line to a neutral country and freedom.

Working for the resistance was extremely dangerous; the Nazi occupation authorities imposed severe penalties on anyone acting against them, and, with German intelligence agents infiltrating the networks and the possibility of being betrayed by unsympathetic neighbors, it was impossible to know who to trust...

Dairy farmer *Tinus Veraart* was a member of the Dutch Resistance and a volunteer on the section of an escape and evasion line that passed Allied airmen over the border and into Belgium. In 1927, he had built Gerda Hoeve, an impressive farmhouse in the 'Amsterdam tradition,' on his land in the small village of Schijf, very close to the Belgian border. Here, Tinus hid evading airmen until arrangements had been made with the Belgian resistance, and then they were helped across the border, just 100 meters behind the farmhouse.

Tinus's two sons were also in the Dutch Resistance. Martijn, the eldest, had been studying economics at Tilburg University, but his studies had ended when the war came to the Netherlands, so he returned home and found temporary work at the Town Hall while sorting documents and maps to help those hiding from the Germans. His brother, Jef, was a guide on the evasion line and collected the evading airmen and brought them to Gerda Hoeve, and then handed them over to his Belgian counterparts, known as the 'White Brigade,' in Essen.

On the 4th of September 1944, it became clear that Hitler was losing the war. German troops based in the Netherlands were disappearing south, and with the large Belgian port of Antwerp liberated, the Dutch were hopeful for a swift end to Nazi rule. Tinus and his family cautiously breathed a sigh of relief, thinking their risky role in the resistance was coming to an end.

That very next day, however, three fugitives appeared at the farmhouse door. These men were not British or American airmen. However, they were wearing German army uniforms. At first, Tinus was terrified; had someone betrayed him? Were they coming to arrest him? But no, they were deserters, unhappy and disillusioned in the *Wehrmacht* and desperate to go home.

They were *Volksdeutsche* (Ethnic Germans), young men from countries that had been invaded by Hitler's forces, such as Czechoslovakia and Poland, that had been drafted into the German Army. The *Wehrmacht* viewed these men as inferior to German-born soldiers; they were rarely promoted and were used for the worst roles in the military. The *Volkesdeutsche* soldiers were generally unhappy and did not trust the German officers.

Tinus did not hesitate for long. He would take these three into hiding just as he had helped all the Allied airmen that had come to his door. Hiding Germans, even if they were Polish-born, was even more dangerous than helping Allied evaders- the Nazis would certainly punish anyone sheltering deserters, and the resistance could take a dim view of Tinus using his valuable resources to hide the enemy, no matter how opposed to Hitler they said they were.

He hid the three men in his grain silo, hoping it wouldn't be for long, but sadly the liberation the Dutch had hoped for was not forthcoming. It would be weeks before the Netherlands was finally free.

The three fugitives did their best to help the family that was sheltering them. After nightfall, when no one would see, they worked on the farm. One of them, Joachim Tometzki, was a similar age to Tinus's son Jef and he talked to him about his experiences, how he had been forced to fight for his country's enemy, and how much he missed his home and his family.

On the 26th of October, the area around Schijf was finally liberated by British forces, and Tinus handed his three *Volksdeutsche* evaders over to them, hoping they would soon be home.

Many years later, after Tinus had passed away, Joachim Tometzki returned to Gerda Hoeve to thank the family that had saved his life. Jef was delighted to see his old friend and asked what had happened to him since the war ended.

Joachim told him that because he had served in the German Army, he had not been allowed to return to Poland, which had become one of the Soviet states after the war. It was a great sadness that he would never be able to visit his homeland or see his parents and other family. He had settled in Belgium and had a family, but he always carried this sense of loss. Despite this, he did find some comfort in the selfless actions of the Veraart family and the lasting friendship he shared with Jef.

Chapter 18

The Warrior Women

Although women most certainly played their part in the Second World War, their contribution to both the Allied and Axis military forces was limited. Their service was restricted to non-combat duties, supporting the war effort, and even fulfilling some defense roles, such as manning heavy anti-aircraft artillery guns. One exception was the remarkable Russian women who served with the 588th Night Bomber Regiment (later known as the 46th "Taman" Guards Night Bomber Aviation Regiment) of the Soviet Air Forces, the first women officially allowed to engage in combat.

By 1941, the Soviet Union had been ravaged by war. Hitler's forces had launched a massive operation to conquer the immense country, and they were perilously close to taking Moscow. The Red Army was struggling in the face of the onslaught; the situation was becoming increasingly desperate.

It was at this time that Major Marina Raskova, the famous Russian aviatrix (who was as famous in the East as Amelia Earhart was in the West), approached Stalin with a request to form a female combat unit. She had received letters from women all over her country, many of whom had lost brothers or loved ones in the fighting and wanted to serve.

Stalin, who had great respect for Major Raskova, gave her orders to form three all-female air force units, and these airwomen were to be tasked with dropping bombs and returning fire. She quickly began to assemble her teams, and with more than 2,000 applications, she selected 400 women for each unit. Her recruits were young, aged between 17 and 26, and many were students.

They began their training at the Engels School of Aviation, just outside Stalingrad - and it was an extremely intense program. Each had to become a proficient pilot, navigator, maintenance engineer, and ground crew in a matter of months. As well as coping with the pressure of learning these skills, the women faced prejudice and harassment from men who were dismissive of Major Raskova's airwomen and didn't believe they could do much to help the Soviet war effort.

The new regiment was given outdated Polikarpov Po-2 biplanes, light, two-seater crop dusters that were hardly designed for combat. They were constructed from plywood frames and stretched canvas panels with open cockpits that offered no protection. The uniforms were just as inadequate; second-hand men's uniforms with too-large boots that the women had to stuff with rags to try and make them fit.

The little wooden planes could not manage the extra weight of parachutes, and the Soviet Air Forces could not afford to equip them with radar and wireless equipment, so the women relied on much more basic equipment; stopwatches, torches, maps, and compasses.

Although the planes were incredibly basic and their maximum speed was slower than the German aircraft they were pitched against, the Polikarpovs proved very agile with skillful handling and could take off and land almost anywhere. When they were attacked, they were forced to dive, and few carried guns (due to the expense and scarcity of ammunition). Because they were so vulnerable, the regiment operated at night.

Flying in an open aircraft in the dark added a further challenge due to the extremely cold, freezing weather conditions. The biting wind made the planes so icy that simply touching the frames with an ungloved hand would take the skin away.

Each plane flew with a pilot at the front and a navigator behind her. They carried just two bombs, one under each wing (the small aircraft could not withstand the weight of any more), and the regiment sent out up to forty a night. The crews flew back between runs to re-arm and re-fuel. The first mission, on the 28th of June 1942, struck the headquarters of the invading German forces and was a great success; the regiment used a tactic by which the first Polikarpovs went in to alert the enemy and, once their spotlights were searching the dark skies, the later planes would idle their engines then stealthily glide to the target and release the bombs. This technique caused their aircraft to make a distinctive whooshing sound that reminded the Germans of a sweeping broom, and since the flyers were women, they called this formidable force the *Nachthexen* - 'night witches.'

And the German forces hated - and feared - these 'night witches.' They were too small to be picked up by radar, and since they didn't use wireless equipment, they couldn't find them on radio locators either. There were rumors that these daredevil women were criminals that the Russians had sent to fight on the front line and that they had been given injections to enable them to see in the dark. Any German flyer that managed to shoot one down was automatically awarded Hitler's Iron Cross.

The airwomen flew more than 30,000 operations and dropped more than 20,000 tons of bombs on German targets and fulfilled a crucial role in the Soviet defenses. They were fiercely proud of their service and of what they achieved. Throughout the war, the regiment lost around thirty pilots, including Major Raskova, on the 4th of January 1943. She was given a state funeral, and her ashes were buried in the Kremlin.

The Night Witches' last flight was recorded on the 4th of May 1945, within 60 km (50 miles) of Berlin, days before Germany made their surrender. Back in Russia, despite their contribution to the defeat of Hitler, the little Polikarpov aircraft were considered too slow to take part in Stalin's victory parade even though the regiment was the most decorated unit in the Soviet Air Forces.

The women who served in the 588th Night Bomber Regiment proved their worth, and in the face of prejudice and with every disadvantage (poor quality aircraft and equipment), they demonstrated that women were just as capable of fighting the enemy as their male counterparts. Although the regiment was disbanded the following year, it helped to start a pathway for women wanting to serve in all roles in the military.

Chapter 19

A Better Scientist

Auschwitz, also known as Auschwitz-Birkenau, was the largest Nazi concentration and death camp. Opened in 1940 and located in southern Poland, it was initially formed as a detention center for political prisoners that opposed Hitler, but it grew into a complex of camps. There, Jewish people and other groups considered enemies of the Nazi states, including Polish and Russian prisoners of war, the Sinai and Roma (gypsies), Jehovah's Witnesses, and homosexuals, were exterminated, often in gas chambers, or made to work in slave labor.

Hans Wilhelm Münch was training to be a doctor when Hitler came to power in Germany. Like a lot of people, he joined the Nazi party because it was becoming impossible to get a job without being a member.

He specialized in bacteriological research, but when war broke out, he began practicing general medicine, treating patients in his hometown in Bavaria, and, as a doctor, he was not expected to join the armed services. The German propaganda and the German public's enthusiastic support for Hitler made Dr. Münch feel as though he should be doing more, "... I thought if all others risked their lives for Germany, then it wasn't right for a young person like me to live as I did with a family... with everything you could hope for when times were bad," and he tried to join the military without success.

By chance, he met Dr. Bruno Weber, an old friend who worked for the government, and told him that he wanted to do more for the German war effort. This friend said he could arrange for Dr. Münch to join the SS (the *Schutzstaffel* or 'protection squadron' was a powerful and feared organization, similar to a military force, commanded by Heinrich Himmler).

Once he had joined, he was told he was to be posted near Krakow. "Nobody said anything about a concentration camp," he recalled in later years. Although he had heard of the camp at Dachau, nothing could have prepared him for what he saw when he arrived at Auschwitz with his wife. They were so shocked his wife could not bring herself to stay, but Dr. Münch had to take up his position at the Hygiene Institute of the Waffen SS, about 3km outside the concentration camp. There, he was to work in bacteriological research under his friend, Dr. Weber.

He quickly learned about Auschwitz and what was happening there and was made to sign various documents binding him to secrecy. The Nazi authorities did not want the outside world to know what was being done there. Dr. Münch could not understand how his friend could stay and accept it.

From the beginning, Dr. Münch was not like the other Nazis. One prisoner said he was "friendly, showed a personal interest in people, never humiliated anyone." He was working on experiments with typhus, and when a company of 100 prisoners marched into the institute, he went to introduce himself and shake hands with them despite his colleagues telling him not to.

When he was informed that he would be expected to go into the camp each week to 'make selections' - decide who would go to the gas chambers, who would be experimented upon, and who would be put to work, Dr. Münch was horrified and told the Chief of Medical Staff, "No. I cannot do it. I will not do it, whatever the consequences," and he was removed from that horrible, inhuman task.

Some people imprisoned at Auschwitz were subjected to barbaric experiments by a medical team led by Josef Mengele, and Dr. Münch worked alongside him. He quickly understood that the poor prisoners that had been treated by Mengele went to the gas chambers when he had finished with them and, unable to accept such cruelty, Dr. Münch devised a program of his own 'experiments'; a series of tests which did not harm these people but instead protected them and kept them alive.

After the war ended, Dr. Münch was identified as one of the medical staff at Auschwitz and was accused of war crimes at a trial at Krakow. Several witnesses spoke of his kindnesses and his refusal to participate in the selections. He was acquitted and became known as the 'good man of Auschwitz' and "a human being in an SS uniform," and he testified at the Auschwitz trial at Frankfurt before returning to Bavaria and continuing his career in medicine.

In retirement, he was approached by survivors of Auschwitz, and he agreed to meet with them and discuss his role and actions. Then in 1995 - the 50th anniversary of the camp's liberation, he returned to Auschwitz and signed a public declaration testifying what had happened there and that such inhumanity should never be allowed to happen again, which was very important to the survivors of the Holocaust as some researchers had started to express some doubts about it.

There are people who believe that Dr. Münch could have done more to help the prisoners at Auschwitz, and, despite witnesses speaking out in his defense, there have been suggestions that he had been involved in helping Mengele's experiments. In his final years, Dr. Münch made some controversial remarks, but by then, his mental health was poor, and he had been diagnosed with Alzheimer's disease.

He was never able to forget the horrors of Auschwitz, however. When Holocaust survivor Eva Kor, who had suffered from the effects of Mengele's experiments throughout her life, spoke to him about her experiences, he told her that he wanted to make amends for anything he had had a part in. He found it difficult to bear his terrible memories, and when she asked him about the gas chambers, he said, "This is the nightmare I live with."

This story demonstrates how we should always try to do the right thing by others, or we may have great regrets later in life.

Chapter 20

Airdrop from Above

The final story actually takes place just after WW2, but we liked it so much that we wanted to include it anyway. It seems a fitting and heartwarming way to end the book.

WHEN THE SECOND World War ended, the Allies had very different ideas about the future of the countries of Europe. The Western Allies believed they should eventually be free to rule themselves in the spirit of democracy, but Stalin had other ideas. He wanted to absorb the Eastern European nations into a state ruled over by an extended Soviet Union. The country of Germany was actually divided into four zones, a Soviet-occupied zone, an American-occupied zone, a British-occupied zone, and a French-occupied zone! Berlin, the capital, was located within the Soviet zone, but it was agreed that it should also be divided into four.

The Soviet Union and the Western Allies had always shared an uneasy relationship; they had defeated Hitler by forcing him to fight on two fronts, but they had very little in common other than a common enemy.

Despite having agreed to divide Berlin, the relationship between the East and the West quickly deteriorated after the war, and the Russians began to feel threatened by the presence of Western troops and the people in West Berlin and thus within the new Eastern bloc.

In June of 1948, Stalin ordered his forces to blockade roads, railways, and waterways to West Berlin. The intention was that it would be impossible for the people living there to get any food or other essential supplies, and the American, British, and French forces would be driven back from the city.

The Western Allies, however, were not prepared to leave and, for a year, ferried 2.3 million tons of food and fuel from airbases in West Germany by large, mainly military aircraft. This 'Operation Vittles' became known as the Berlin Airdrop.

Colonel *Gail Seymour Halvorsen*, a pilot in the USAAF, was assigned to fly C-47 and C-54 aircraft during the Berlin Airdrop. He enjoyed being stationed overseas and liked to spend his time sightseeing when he wasn't on duty. One day, he was using his cine camera to film aircraft taking off and landing at Tempelhof airbase in West Berlin when he noticed about thirty young children behind the wire fences that surrounded the airfield. He went to have a chat with them.

They were there to watch the planes, and all loaded up with food. They were very hungry, many of the people of Berlin who had spent years living with limited, rationed supplies of food were now starving, but their excitement and gratitude touched Gail. They said to him, "When the weather gets so bad that you cannot land, don't worry about us. We can get by on little food, but if we lose our freedom, we might never get it back!"

He took a couple of sticks of chewing gum from his pocket and handed them to them. The children broke it into as many tiny pieces as they could so they could all have a share, and those who didn't get any sniffed the wrappers. Gail watched them, feeling sad that he hadn't any more to give them. They had so little, and their short lives had been so blighted by war he wanted to do something for them. He told them that he would get plenty of gum for them and that he would drop it out of his plane the following day. "How will we know if it is your plane?" The children asked in delight. Gail said that he would wiggle his wings - just as he had done back in America in 1941 for his parents when he had qualified as a pilot.

That evening he and his crew pooled their candy rations to drop the next day. Concerned that the sweet treats were quite a weight and might injure the children waiting for them, he divided them into parcels and attached makeshift parachutes out of pocket handkerchiefs so they would safely float to the ground.

The next morning, the little parcels were dropped for the children outside the airfield as Gail flew his plane over them. For the next three weeks, Gail's crew continued packing their candy and dropping it for the thankful little Berliners waiting with hungry anticipation below.

Large crowds of children started gathering, waiting for their 'candy bomber.' The Airlift Commander, when he heard about Gail's scheme, decided to expand it and launched 'Operation Little Vittles' was officially launched on 22 September 1948.

When reports of the American airmen dropping their chocolate and gum for the poor children of Berlin were published in US newspapers, huge quantities of candy - and handkerchiefs - were donated by the public as well as gifts of money, in order to support the operation. Confectionery manufacturers wanted to play a role, too, and by November of that year, there were so many donations that it became a national project, and Gail's squadron was dropping treats every day.

Gail, who had been known as 'Uncle Wiggly' to the children of Berlin, was also known as 'The Chocolate

Uncle,' the 'Chocolate Flyer,' and the 'Gum Drop Kid.' He returned back to the United States in January 1949, but the operation continued, and by the time the Berlin Aircraft ended, more than 23 tons of candy had been dropped by more than 250,000 parachutes.

The children of Berlin sent letters and drawings to thank the people of America, not just for the candy but for their compassion taking them, the sons and daughters of their former enemies, to their hearts.

THE END

Conclusion

These stories, from South Dakota to Japan, have taught us many important lessons. They've demonstrated the importance of helping our enemy, bravery, doing the right thing, and so much more. We've seen how important having hope is, whether it comes in the form of a Dog or a Brown Bear. We've read about the power of love, and how it can be rekindled decades and decades later. We've seen Miracles from God & the beauty of forgiveness.

We really hope you liked this book, and hope that you learned something from it - whether that be an important moral, or simply some new vocabulary and interesting WWII facts!

If you and your children enjoyed reading this book, we'd be very grateful for a 5* review on Amazon. It

Conclusion

helps our new small business more than you'd ever know!

Yours,

KLG History

Also by KLG History

We plan to publish lots more short stories soon. Be sure to follow us on Amazon to be notified ahead of new releases.

www.ingramcontent.com/pod-product-compliance
Lightning Source LLC
Chambersburg PA
CBHW012005090526
44590CB00026B/3887